SQUATCHIN'

STUDY GUIDE AND FIELD HANDBOOK FOR TRACKING SASQUATCH

GARY AND WENDY SWANSON

Sasquatch image on the cover is courtesy of
Edward Monge

Published by Swanson Literary Group
ISBN: 9781705616673

Other books by the authors:

Bigfoot Uncovered: Finding Sasquatch
Sasquatch Encounters: True Tales Of Bigfoot
They Saw Sasquatch: Close Encounters With Bigfoot
Tracking Sasquatch
Sasquatch!: Reports From the Field
Bigfoot Adventures
Hiking Sasquatch Country: Best Hikes In Southern Oregon

Skinwalkers Shapeshifters and Native American Curses
We Survived Native American Witches, Curses & Skinwalkers
The Last Skinwalker: The Avenging Witch Of The Navajo Nation

CONTENTS

	Introduction	7
1	Preparation for Squatchin'	9
2	Weighing In; Mystery Solved!	14
3	Secrets for Hiking Sasquatch Country	19
4	Color Me Blah	23
5	Increasing Your Odds for Finding Sasquatch	25
6	Sounds of Silence	29
7	Sasquatch Goes Airborne	32
8	On the Sasquatch Trail	37
9	Tracking Sasquatch	41
10	Sasquatch Facts	50
11	Let's Talk "Scat"	58
12	The Eyes Have It	60
13	Bigfoot Telegraph	63
14	Another Sasquatch Deception	71
15	Photographing Sasquatch	76
16	Capturing Sasquatch	83
17	Hibernation; Two Schools of Thought	86
18	Sasquatchs' Hidden Highways	88
19	Sasquatch Hunters	93
20	Serious Squatchin'	94
	Field Notes	102

INTRODUCTION

Cryptozoology is the study of animals that are rumored to exist. Such animals are called "cryptids."

"Sasquatch" was named in the 1920's by journalist J.W. Burns, as a common denominator for the myriad of names being used by so many people, and it stuck!

The name was derived from the word "Sesquae" from the Halq'eméylem language. Sasquatch finally received official status on September 27, 2002 when Doctor Jane Goodall, the renowned primatologist and conservationist said regarding Sasquatch, "I tell you that I am sure they exist."

Sounds that are attributed to Sasquatch are: loud screams, whoops, wales, whistles, grunts, intense screeches, and tooth clicking (grinding teeth).

An adult Sasquatch has long arms, disproportionately broad shoulders and medium-long legs; a four-foot stride, leaving 16-inch footprints for the average adult males.

In collecting material and interviewing sources for this handbook, we researched extensively throughout the heart of Sasquatch country. We consulted the experts who have lived among these fascinating creatures, and from them, learned the "secrets" of how these reclusive beings have for so long existed in relative anonymity.

This handbook contains a composite of everything that makes Sasquatch so unique among the animal kingdom. It is possible that Sasquatch quite likely watched Christopher Columbus first invade their home back in the year 1492!

There are ancient stone carvings bearing the exact likeness of Sasquatch creatures in perfect detail lying hidden underwater on the rocky walls of the Columbia River that separates the states of Oregon and Washington. These images were unfortunately covered with water by the construction of The Dalles Dam. These carvings are evidence that the early Native Americans must have considered them as sort of deities!

Our first Sasquatch experience happened when we retired to Southern Oregon, and after that event, we met countless others who shared their experiences with us. This began our publishing a series of books.

Over the years, the habits and lives of these mysterious creatures became a collection of facts about their habits and their clever means of quickly disappearing when discovered.

PREPARATION FOR SQUATCHIN'

When hiking in Sasquatch Country, we are constantly reminded that we are traveling through wild country that is home to numerous wild animals, such as coyotes, cougars, fox, bobcats, roving wolf packs, bears, and of course, the Sasquatch itself! All of the named animals have at one time or another attacked humans when startled, and some even stalk people purposely.

The best advice we can give is to be constantly alert; never reach into holes or step into caves or slot canyons before conducting a careful inspection first!

Since one's outdoor wardrobe is a matter of personal choice, we offer a few suggestions before you enter the world of Sasquatch.

Dress as "blah" as you can. Clothes that blend with the outdoors are best. That's why so many camouflage-patterned clothes are available. You are likely to be less conspicuous if you also wear softer soled hiking shoes or boots. No colognes, perfumes, and definitely no cigarettes!

As an old military sniper friend said to me regarding the enemy's propensity for smoking, "First I'd smell 'em coming and dig in, then they'd finally come into view, and then I would make another notch on my rifle butt!"

Sasquatch don't carry guns yet, but the cigarettes will forecast your arrival! Besides, fire is the biggest fear of all forest dwellers.

Wear hiking shoes that don't "clump" with every step. Those hard-soled clodhoppers may be your sporting goods store's "best sellers," but the first time those hard soles send a rock pinging into the air, that Sasquatch will disappear until you are long past.

Now, what about jackets? That comfortable jacket that felt so great at seven o'clock in the morning will soon be a terrible discomfort when the sun is high and it's ninety degrees on the trail.

Sure, you can tie it around your waist and spend the entire day in discomfort, or if you're returning by the same route you can always hide it alongside the trail and recover it on the way back.

Think about this one carefully, because even the constant swish-swish of a jacket worn tied around you can sound much louder to a nearby Sasquatch. It's not surprising as to how many jackets we have seen alongside mountain trails over the years. Plan your wardrobe around the weather forecast.

Now, let's talk about camera gear. Carrying the added bulk of tripods and telephoto lenses on the chance of a photo op with Sasquatch will likely only cause misery. Besides, Sasquatch seldom poses for family photos, and if you think you may get an opportunity for a distance shot; forget it!

Sasquatch is hardly ever spotted in the open. Those areas, he travels after sundown and in early, early dawn.

Should you get that million-dollar opportunity, you had better hope you're carrying a simple point and shoot in your hand or around your neck.

Based on the stories of hundreds, we wish we could offer better advice, but these critters are just too cautious.

At best you can hope for a quick shot, but in all likelihood, your camera shut itself off to conserve its battery and you are likely to get a "see 'ya later" shot of its backside. Then you can have fun trying to convince everyone that it isn't a shot of your drunken Uncle Larry in his father's 1930 full-length fur coat!

Now that we've hit on the negatives, let's address the important items.

A first aid kit will be a blessing, as even a small cut or bruise on an ankle can become sheer misery by the end of the day.

We highly recommend rolling off a long strip of duct tape around a pencil or stick for convenience of conserving space, because it will do everything from wrapping a wound with your shirt tail to a myriad of other uses. Even securing a loosened sole of a hiking shoe can save the day. It also works to tie sticks around a sprained ankle; a comforting fact when you are miles from where you parked!

Duct tape can also help construct an emergency travois. Most of us never intentionally roam so far out, but being hot on a set of Sasquatch tracks can make one lose all track of time; true story!

A knife is a necessity for obvious reasons, and matches are always comforting for emergencies. It gets awfully cold at night in Sasquatch's backyard!

Your intention may tend to lead toward the establishment of a "base camp" so the Sasquatch will come to you, but it will not happen. Once you enter the forest, your only chance of spotting a Sasquatch will be to walk up on one. Sasquatch does not seem to make very many mistakes when it travels, but the sightings always seem to happen when someone walks up on one when it is concentrating on something.

Perhaps it is because human odors carry to Sasquatch, as the Bigfoot can itself smell quite foul if we are downwind of it! In all likelihood, Sasquatch feels the same about us.

Now let's talk about water. Since one never really can guess at how much we will need, carry plenty. You can always dump the excess anytime, but never dare to take a chance of too little going in. You cannot count on taking water from streams, and emergencies could add a lot of time to your trip, so you'll be glad to have it. If hiking with dogs, bring an even greater excess, and sandwich bags for them to drink from.

Take a few high-energy, protein snacks for everyone in your group, including the dogs; you may end up spending more time in the wilds than you had planned.

Also remember a good map, a GPS system and a pen. There is a place for notes and coordinates in this guide book; and be aware that signals can often be confusing in the mountains. Record strange sounds and locations for later research.

Be extremely careful, as mistakes in this terrain are seldom forgiven and can result in serious danger. Many hikers in areas where bear are plentiful, make it a habit to attach small bells to their clothing and carry whistles.

Be aware of the trail you are taking, and when deep in the more wild areas, keep an eye out for animal tracks and scat. Bear droppings will be noticeable by a large percentage of berries and animal fur; while cougar scat will contain some animal fur, and also small "bells and whistles!" Just kidding; have fun Squatchin'!

WEIGHING IN; MYSTERY SOLVED!

Our years of research and countless interviews with so many of our contributors across the North American continent, who have encountered Sasquatch, left a lingering question which until only recently remained unanswered; the mystery of just how much the adult male Sasquatch really weighs has been speculated at being in the neighborhood of 500 pounds, and oftentimes a lot more!

We have, for years, accepted these estimates to be reasonably accurate, but largely because of the comparisons with the gorilla, and the opinions of those learned individuals and various well-respected members of academia. Who among us "Squatchers" would question the opinions of such respected individuals?

Throughout all of the reports we analyzed from those people across the continent who had actual encounters with the Sasquatch, that thread of doubt lingered until only recently. Making a concerted effort to clear up this mystery; we had to solve the questionable sighting of Sasquatch keeping lookout from the tops of pine trees.

Every mystery about the Sasquatch footprints in areas where deer tracks and cougar prints alike mingled one atop the other with little difference in the depth of the impressions was evident. The depth of the Sasquatch tracks did not indicate that there was that greater depth enough to verify it being that much heavier.

This gave us cause to suspect the fact that the Sasquatch weight had been overestimated and maybe enhanced by fiction writers. Thus, began our reassessment of our "mystery beast," and after many discussions with our contributors, we have reached the following conclusions.

We know that the hair fiber of the Bigfoot is made of highly tensile, hollow hairs; the consistency of which acts as insulation against severe cold, yet fine enough to also cool the animal in the summer heat. We further concluded that many people have seemingly added a bit to every Sasquatch encounter; and the animal has grown in stature and power, more by enthusiasm than reality.

Our recent conclusions are that the Sasquatch can reach somewhat over seven feet in height, although the thickness of hair on its head and neck can make it seem a lot taller. The Bigfoot has an extremely strong bone structure, and that fact, along with the consistency of its hair, misleads observers as to the animals' weight. We believe the Sasquatch weight seldom exceeds 250 pounds, with the rare exception estimated to go as high as 330 pounds at most. Far less than heretofore estimated; it makes perfect sense when one compares the almost total absence of any deep footprints associated with the higher weight estimates so often reported.

Many of the early plaster casts of Bigfoot tracks were admittedly fakes, as were so many stories about Sasquatch being a ferocious giant! Although it made for good copy at the time, many of these exaggerated falsehoods have carried forward in today's world and intermingled with our current studies.

We know that this creature is neither the vicious nor the horribly large terror it has previously been portrayed to be. The lighter weight of the adults gives credence to the shallow footprints normally found near Sasquatch sightings, and in all likelihood, is the reason for the almost total absence of any more plaster footprint casts appearing these days from reputable sources.

Our conclusions also answer the even bigger mystery that we have long pondered; that is, how could such a heavy animal ever keep lookout from treetops as we know the Sasquatch so often does? The lighter weight of the animal makes such observation entirely plausible, coupled with the fact that the role of "observer," usually falls to the noticeably smaller-statured Sasquatch when traveling in family units.

Also clearing up another mystery that we were more recently informed of from contributors in several Eastern states and from several large-acreage ranches in the Western mountains of the country; four separate contributors had reported instances of Sasquatch being observed swinging through the trees on their properties for a rapid descent in the thickly forested acreages below. When we first heard of this (never before reported) activity, we held off publishing these reports until we received several more that prompted further study and investigation. It seems that there were entire families of Sasquatch living on a few huge properties, and the owners waited to report until they checked out our promise of total anonymity protection for our story submitters. Once our security measures had been verified, we received our first report where Sasquatch were observed in a flooded area in the Eastern USA as they swung in well-measured stretches from tree to tree across the huge, waterlogged areas!

Shortly after publishing that event, we received two more reports from Western cattle ranchers who reported the Sasquatch traveling long distances through their forests by well-timed swinging, arm-over-arm as they rapidly proceeded across rugged areas with great coordination!

The one unanswered question that still gave us concern was how these huge beasts could so quickly travel Tarzan-like without breaking branches and falling. Certainly, pine branches are resilient and super-strong, but we, at that time, were still under the premise that Sasquatch was a three or four-hundred-pound animal. Now that we have reached the conclusion that Bigfoot is not really all that heavy, it makes perfect sense and validates our belief in the sincerity of our story submitters.

Our suspicions of some stories submitted to us, have in the past, kept us from publishing certain stories out of caution that they didn't seem credible are now coming out of our "pending" file cabinet for further review. Since we have concluded, for the record, that Sasquatch is not the four-hundred-pound monster that lurks in the dark mountains, we can see that there is cause to reinvestigate those submissions that may perhaps shed even more light on the subject of "Squatchin'!"

Remember, when you're out hiking, the large pile of leaves in the top of the distant tree may not be a squirrel or eagle's nest at all; it just may be a Sasquatch!

Good Squatchin'!

INVITATION:

If you have had a personal encounter or sighting of a Sasquatch that you would like to see published in our next book, please send the details and any accompanying photos to:

swanliterary@gmail.com

Please include a "pen name" if you do not want your name revealed. If your story is published, you will receive a signed copy of the book as our thanks. We look forward to hearing from you!

SECRETS FOR HIKING SASQUATCH COUNTRY

Most visitors to our scenic areas, when hiking alongside our lakes and streams never really expect to encounter or even see a Sasquatch.

This is an assumption based on experiences, as the Sasquatch are very much like the cougars, bear, coyote and other predatory animals that we know are out there, but it's the old "out of sight, out of mind" theory that allows most people to not be disappointed if they don't see one, as they are convinced from the beginning that they will not.

Sasquatch are very much like other predatory animals that seldom travel where they can be seen by other creatures, and especially by humans.

Humans are the one species that will never leave the other animals alone; if they see most any wild animal, they immediately overreact and cause such a commotion that they alert every living thing in a half-mile radius at a minimum!

Passing through any forested area can bring a real bonus to your hike if you maintain as strict a silence as you possibly can. Be alert and you will very soon realize what the sound, or lack of sound is normal for the area you are in.

Once you learn the norm, it will be easy to pick up on any sounds that may indicate a change. This change can be as simple as a whoosh of air similar to a distant sneeze.

Do not be too quick to dismiss any sound that doesn't fit within the normal parameters that you have assimilated into. The sudden swoosh of air may be a lot more significant when you learn that the Sasquatch is known to sneeze quite often. Some experts and experienced observers feel that the Bigfoot animals do so in order to clear their rather large nasal passages. They also are known to snort or sneeze to clean their large sinus cavities from a buildup of pollens and other airborne particles. Whenever they detect the smell of humans, which is unlike any forest dwellers that Sasquatch in familiar with, they are known to quietly sneeze in order to better sense the direction the odor is coming from.

When you hear such a sound when you are hiking through the forest, it is your cue to immediately drop to the ground and get into an unstrained, comfortable position. Now you just need to turn up your alertness level, because you may have an upcoming Sasquatch encounter! Do not be in too much of a hurry to resume your hike, as Sasquatch has a canny way of sitting patiently and just listening and sniffing the air.

That sneezing or wheezing sound is a good indicator that your scent may have been picked up, and the animal has cleared its sensors, so it is now analyzing the air. If it doesn't catch any further scent, it may, out of its natural propensity to inspect every smell, be moving slowly about in an effort to test the ever-changing winds. Your odds will be increased dramatically if you remain stationary, and preferably sitting on the ground.

Squatting positions end too quickly, because we can't maintain such uncomfortable stances for long. Sit comfortably down and stay alert, as Sasquatch may be coming to you!

Just as the Sasquatch will turn, tip its head and occasionally snort when trying to identify smells, it acts an awful lot like the radar system for sounds as well.

Going back to those "wheezy" sounds that we often attributed to grouse and other birds, we now recall several instances where they were most likely to have been created by Sasquatch. As so often happened then, our dogs picked up on the sounds and our excited actions, and would often let out a bark or growl that instantly warned every animal within a half a mile that humans and dogs were present.

Looking back at those crucial moments, we should have simply given up and gone home. Our discovery period was over!

Now, there are times when a Sasquatch will, instead of pounding a tree with a branch or rock, let out a sort of whistle that sounds somewhat like a loud bird chirp.

If you hear that sound, we recommend that you drop to the ground and stay perfectly still. Remain sitting for at least ten minutes. Oftentimes the chirp or whistle will receive an answer of a similar sound almost on the heels of the first one.

This happens most often when two or more Sasquatch are traveling through the forest in a common direction. It is their way to stay closely connected, but seldom if ever, do they travel side by side unless one is wounded and needs assistance. The Sasquatch do not seem to be particularly interested in companionship outside of their immediate family.

We have observed Sasquatch encampments from a distance away, and there is a decided lack of communication and comradery. We know that these animals will band together in large colonies at certain times during the year; which we suspect to be tied in with mating purposes, but there appears to be a total lack of gathering for protection a group might provide.

If danger threatens, it is generally from hunters or hikers, and then the comradery is cut short and they kind of disappear. It's like, "every Sasquatch for itself."

These animals may be in a human-like shape, but from appearances, they do not have even a thread of mutual cooperation for their common good. These strange creatures almost totally ignore others in their gatherings.

A scientist and cryptozoologist who once accompanied us on a two-month study said the Sasquatch reminded him of "a den of snakes," with their close contact and mingling, yet with an almost total disregard for the others presence!

COLOR ME BLAH

People continually ask when heading into Sasquatch Country, "What colors should I wear?" We put the word out a while ago to try and get a feel for what most people think is best for "Squatchin'." No one knows for certain if the Sasquatch is able to distinguish colors from one another, or if they only can differentiate between various shades of light and dark.

Reports from the field are quite varied as to whether or not any particular color either attracts or offends these giants. We received such a variance of opinions and encounters where it did not seem as if the animals had any color perception at all. Most contributors have responded with the suggestions of keeping the color of clothing down to greens, browns and blacks. Whether or not there is a Sasquatch color spectrum, a good rule of thumb is to dress sort of on the "ugly side" as one responder said. Above all else, we personally recommend that you dress so you blend into the greens and browns of the environment you are in.

Animals, for the most part, seem to have a propensity toward color blindness, as evidenced by the fact that deer, elk and bear hunters wear reds and oranges for their personal protection so they aren't shot by other hunters; the animals do not seem to notice.

On the other hand, when you observe mating among bird species, the males with the most beautiful plumage attract the first females.

Sasquatch are not really attention-drawn to any visual stimulation; however, the general consensus is to dress "camo" just in case.

The only warning would be to avoid wearing any red or orange, as these colors signal to any experienced forest dwellers that there will soon be a massive encroachment by hordes of "gun toting" hunters. That's the scare you don't want to impart; you may just convince the entire forest that deer season has begun! Kind of like when we were kids and the first clown and elephant posters began to appear on local light poles; we didn't have to read the words to know the circus was coming!

INCREASING YOUR ODDS FOR FINDING SASQUATCH

Humans definitely do not fit well in the forest environments. The main reason is that we seem to be constantly communicating with one another. We talk continually and jabber everywhere we go, even while walking through our beautiful forests.

We can readily identify with this hard-to-break habit. It's almost as if we operate like that old car you're afraid to turn off, because it may never start again.

Most of us spend our days communicating on our jobs and in our personal lives, so shutting it down and succumbing to the silence of the outdoors is alarmingly unnatural. When hiking in areas where there is still a cellphone connection, it is ludicrous to meet hikers walking along, carrying on conversations on their cellphones as though they are connected to a lifeline that must be kept open.

Hiking and texting do not mix; shut 'em off people and take control of your life again. Enjoy the luxury and beauty of the forest, whose only job is to shelter and protect its denizens; especially the mysterious monster lurking just behind the next tree on your right!

So you won't have any regrets by such a monster jumping out and ripping your throat out, why not enjoy your time in a different world than the one you suffer in all week long? If the Sasquatch wasn't such a docile animal, it could easily have leapt out and taken you home to feed its family!

We have little to fear in most of our forests, but there are quite a number of animals that could be extremely nasty if caught at the wrong time. Take the mama bear with cubs that you must avoid at all costs, the cougar, lynx, gray wolf, maybe rattlesnakes and others.

Depending upon where you live, man is not always superior in a confrontation with animals protecting themselves or their family. Stay alert when you're out of your element. Even small buck deer have the ability to kill you if they wish. Those antlers are shaped for self-defense.

We are of course, simply mentioning these facts, so when you are out of your normal environment, be aware of where you are at present.

So, while on the subject, what if the docile Sasquatch behind the tree up ahead had just been kicked out of its cave home by its mate? What if it also has a horrible toothache from an abscess caused by a broken elk bone? Now, what do you suppose would happen, if in your semi-conscious state, you walk right into this enraged three-hundred-pound animal that's twice your size and ten times meaner and stronger?

I think we can agree that the last thing on this suffering animal's mind at this moment is making a new friend. Had you not been texting; you may have been alert to that large fur coat the kept turning and writhing on the other side of that tree with its' pounding chest protruding a foot beyond the edge and well into your view.

Hopefully this poor, suffering animal, even with all of its pain and anxiety, heard you coming, and out of sheer kindness toward a lesser species, stepped further off the trail and let you pass without ever knowing how close you came! Although this scenario is not likely to occur, be aware that it could. How do we ever know? Who would be around to tell anyone?

Sasquatch can attain the size of a large black bear, only taller. They are seldom violent toward humans, and do not have a propensity toward aggressiveness; "Thank you Mother Nature!"

Even though this often monstrously big animal is quite docile; if angered or threatened, especially if young ones are present, it could easily be a game changer. Compared to most humans, this animal can turn into a monster!

These fascinating creatures live among us, travel the same hiking trails that we do, and yet in almost all cases, we humans often walk within a few feet of them without even knowing they are there. Proof of this is evident from reports we have on file.

Since you are reading this handbook, we assume that you are either in Sasquatch County or planning an adventure, so please prepare properly!

We highly recommend venturing out into the wilds with another set of human eyes to see, discuss and evaluate clues and events that may be misunderstood, so you can compare notes on the spot. If taking a dog, be aware that the Sasquatch have an exceptionally strong fear of these animals, because a dog, by nature, will attack and kill a young Sasquatch or any other species, because it is natural for them. Your odds, if accompanied by a dog, of seeing a Sasquatch will be greatly diminished. On the other hand, the Sasquatch do not seem to particularly fear humans; they just don't apparently have any use for us.

As we walk and enjoy the scenery, we must use every care in where we place each footstep. The simple "ping" of a stone snapping from beneath a hard-soled hiking boot can be heard by an alert Sasquatch a half a block away. You know the old saying about "walking and chewing gum," but now watching where we place each step is a whole new wrinkle.

"Walking without talking," will reveal to you a wonderous assortment of creatures that most people pass right by without ever seeing.

SOUNDS OF SILENCE

Think carefully about this. Have you ever been walking along, listening to the pleasant chorus of crickets and frogs harmonizing in a nearby swamp or stream, when before you get closer than a hundred feet, all goes silent? You have been heard and seen! The tiny swamp dwellers and nearby fields of small inhabitants both heard and saw you from that far away.

Always keep in mind that well before you can even see the pond or swamp, the inhabitants can see you. Reason being, is that their home is well-concealed, revealing only a few signs of the pond's or swamp's presence, where your head and especially hats, show up over their grass and bush covered hideouts before you even have a clue of their lair.

For this reason alone; always walk on the side of the trail as far away from these musical retreats as you can. The secret is to hopefully keep them singing, as the moment that they stop, every forest dweller in the area is now aware of your presence! They don't normally stop their serenading for forest animals, but the total cessation of sound can indicate only one intruder that stops everything; man! When walking on the side of the road or trail away from such a pond, it will also help if you duck down and walk more slowly as well.

Now let's look at a similar scenario where you have taken a break and have sat alongside this pond long enough that the occupants have no longer a sense of danger and they are once again engaged in their musical serenades, when suddenly, the "deafening sound of silence" assaults your eardrums. You carefully crouch somewhat lower, and turning ever so slowly, you find yourself looking directly into the shocked eyes of Sasquatch!

As we are alerted by sounds, we must, when in the forest, be aware of an even more important warning, and that is the absence of sound! The very absence of sound is the most serious alert, as it indicates that whatever the cause, every creature near you is afraid of something that has just arrived on the scene. Maybe it's you; however, if you heard no sound as you approached, you just may have company!

Many animals in our vast forests, swamps, mountains and deserts live by the rather simple fact of either, "kill or be killed." No matter how tall or well positioned on the ground, only the birds have the great advantage of sight. For the ground dwellers, sound is the most important survival tool they possess, and they must know how to interpret every chord and every lack of same.

Most animal species in the wild live under a cloud of apprehension, as they are always in danger of being killed and eaten. Therefore, when we think about sneaking up on Sasquatch for that perfect photo op; as they say, "Ain't gonna happen!"

Here's the picture; you're walking casually along an old rutted road in the dense forest when a slight movement ahead and to your left catches your eye. Then, a large bush blocks your view and once past it, you are eyeball to eyeball with a majestic black-tail buck. You come to a stop, but before you are able to even touch your camera, the deer has vanished. Sound familiar?

When in Sasquatch Country, make a habit of having your camera where you can place your hand on it in a quick second; practice this constantly.

We gave up doing this drill long ago, because our panting dogs make certain that we don't need to bother with a close-up photo of anything wild!

SASQUATCH GOES AIRBORNE

Over the years, we have received several reports from property owners that refer to what we nicknamed, "Sasquatch playing Tarzan!" We accepted these reports for our files, however, we remained reticent regarding these stories, until we received more, almost identical stories from many very credible witnesses.

Several reports from owners of large properties consisting of hundreds of acres of forested lands being left in the "wild" arrived in our mail after some extended rainy periods back east. These huge properties are pretty much left to nature, and in many instances, they are surrounding huge acreages of cropland. These forests act as privacy buffers for many wealthy landowners.

The Sasquatch have been known by the property owners to exist for ages, and they, in many cases, even leave various food items for their "resident Bigfoot" population.

Several reports came to us during a series of devastating rains that caused large areas to remain severely flooded for long periods. The reports we received told of Bigfoot having been observed "swinging from tree to tree" in order to pass from hill to hill across the flooded ground. To quote one of our submitters, "They look like giant, hairy Tarzans, swinging hand over hand from tree to tree with a seemingly well-practiced rhythm."

We gathered from some of our reports coming in from various landowners, that having a family of resident Sasquatch is a sort of status symbol. Some of those who sent letters take great pride in their closely held secret, "creature covens," as one lady said. We had reservations about believing this; however, three separate reports made reference in different ways to this fact that the Sasquatch prefer to not get their "big feet" wet!

Another reference regarding the "Tarzan travel" method came in from a family on a huge acreage out west. The property is mostly forested by evergreens on the surrounding hills, with flat acreage in between where they grow crops.

The owner and his sons were hunting deer on a more remote area of their property, when they walked around a hill and observed a large Sasquatch swinging hand over hand, from one pine tree to another, over a large, steep gully to the valley floor below. They reported that the animal never saw them as it swiftly traversed an area they estimated to be the size of two football fields. They said that the Sasquatch seemed to have a well-practiced gait, and that it must have regularly used this method of travel, since it never once slipped or missed a branch all the way across and down this massive ravine.

The ranchers were surprised that these animals were there long enough to have established visible trails. Even though they had previously seen their huge footprints and were aware of their presence. The ranchers then suggested to us that perhaps the fact that the coyote population was much less that year could possibly be attributed to the Sasquatch presence. Several ranch owners have reported that Sasquatch enjoy meals of coyote!

Another of our submitters owns a large property in Montana, and his family had long been aware of the Sasquatch living in more remote areas of their land and the thousands of acres of government lands adjacent to their vast holdings.

For years, they were aware of a group of Sasquatch living on their property, but they seldom ever found any worn trails, or even more than a rare footprint of the animals, and then, the prints seemed small, like young ones would leave. When they thought more about it, it led to further discussions and concern that the Bigfoot population may be in trouble. This prompted a few of the brothers and cousins conducting a search of the less visited areas on the ranch and into the adjoining government land.

The mystery was solved on the second day, when two riders surprised several Sasquatch as they suddenly rode through a pass between two large hills, and there, they caught by surprise, this group of four Bigfoot who gave away their secret when they took flight!

The four creatures were in a panic as they quickly took to the trees. There they went, hand over hand, swinging quickly without pause from tree to tree, one after the other, and in just over a minute, the ranchers told us they were out of sight in the forest below! After going up close and inspecting a couple of the trees they remembered seeing the animals leap to when they began their descent; they reported the discovery of the bark in those handholds was totally gone, and they could see, following the pathway used that every branch along the line had been worn totally smooth.

It was obvious that this route had not simply been a matter of expedience from the ranchers' sudden appearance, but rather a preferred and much faster way to traverse the distance down to the valley. The group of ranchers were further enlightened by inspecting more carefully, and recalled how the animals had a rhythm of sorts as they would swing in a sort of looping motion from tree to tree.

Further investigation of the area revealed that there also were signs where the rocky slopes were impossible to ascend on foot; there were indications that the Sasquatch also used a network of branches to travel upwards all the way to the top. They indicated that the obvious spots worn for the ascent were much closer together, but the necessity for a long swinging movement to transcend the canyons were still apparent.

Once we became aware of this discovery, we relayed the information to other researchers, and although few had noticed these signs, it answered many questions for quite a large group. We soon received reports from some of these researchers that revisited some of the mountainous areas and treacherous canyons that had once stymied them. They found visible signs of this hand over hand travel on the worn off bark of additional tree branches. As one of our Oregon friends told us; it answered a lot of questions about how the Sasquatch can so quickly scale the sheer cliffs of some of the narrow canyons in the Cascade and Siskiyou mountains.

ON THE SASQUATCH TRAIL

No other animal known to man seems to be as clever as the Sasquatch. We do have a couple of reports of bears, especially Grizzlies, occasionally walking erect with the assist of low hanging tree branches from overhead for their front paws to use to steady their progress.

Why they do this is reasoned by the witnesses; to enable them to better identify sounds and smells that have come on the wind. They will turn in different directions like a radar screen; watching, listening and sniffing the air.

Sasquatch does exactly the same thing without needing the assist of tree branches, although the Bigfoot is known to use these branches to pull itself up to better avail itself of more of the sounds and smells of danger.

This is something to keep in mind while hiking, especially if you are traveling in a more exposed area, such as an open meadow. Constantly scan the forests around you and keep an eye out for a sight that may be slightly out of the ordinary. That dark spot in the upper branches of that deciduous tree may not be a nesting osprey or hawk after all, and instead of a squirrel's nest, perhaps you're staring at a pair of eyes belonging to Sasquatch!

All too often, those otherwise keen observers seem to fall into the acceptance that all nests look similar and ignore the brownish, leaf-colored Sasquatch youngster who spends its childhood spying on other interesting species; like humans.

We were very fortunate to have begun our interest in Sasquatch at a time where fate introduced us to an old-time gold prospector and expert in "all things wilderness!"

We visited quite often over the years, and he taught us how to pan gold, and the conversations that continued during our get togethers began turning to Sasquatch. This was all because of a chance spotting of one when we were panning gold. Otherwise, like so many of the prospector's ilk, the subject may have never have come up, as they seem to prefer their solitude rather than drawing attention of more visitors.

The Sasquatch animals are certainly not revered as one might expect, because of how the long-time mining community protects them, but to the contrary. To the miners, the Sasquatch are a nuisance that they have a mutual respect for, but only because of the frightening alternative; that would be the catastrophic results of word getting out of Sasquatch living in these pristine forests near their prospecting sites. We purposely do not mention our friend's name to honor our pledge to secrecy, because as he says it, "If word of our hairy neighbors ever got out, all hell would break loose and our personal worlds would be destroyed!" We heartily concur, and thus will never reveal their locations. We honor this same pledge to all of our contributors of Sasquatch encounters.

We did learn one secret from our association that was new to us at the time, and it answered a lot of lingering questions. Our friend calls it the "Bigfoot backing up technique." His teaching us this "trick" used by Sasquatch has saved us untold hours ever since.

Adding to his sage advice, he shared his "first rule of Squatchin'." "If it is too good to believe; don't! He went on to explain that if one finds a clear trail of Sasquatch footprints across any area of length other than a very few feet that seems too good to be true; it likely will be. Every time!

Anytime this most secretive and reclusive animal leaves visible footprints, it is because it wants you to find them! The only exception to this rule would be in the unlikely event that it was pursuing game and was close by at that very moment. Otherwise it would have gone back and erased its sign. They really do! This is a heretofore unknown fact, and we were at first skeptical until we received confirming proof shortly thereafter. We have been really appreciative of this information over the years.

Sasquatch could be perceived of having a neatness fetish, because it leaves no discernable evidence of its having been there. This particular scenario answered many questions about the difficulties in tracking this elusive critter, and then we learned what our friend's "backing back" theory was really all about.

Whenever the Sasquatch has, out of necessity, left a visible trail such as in pursuit of a meal or a quick exodus from an area to avoid humans, or to quickly exit because of the sudden appearance of a "cute Squatchita's" father; it will always return to erase its sign. This is why finding a Sasquatch footprint clear enough to make a plaster cast is so rare.

Actually, the experts agree that the Sasquatch have definite knowledge and a fear that man has a genuine thirst for the evidence of their existence; and for this reason, the majority of all Sasquatch footprint casts are quite old, having been taken years back. One may assume that the animals are much more cautious about revealing their presence now that they have reached "celebrity" status!

TRACKING SASQUATCH

Since the primary purpose of this book is to guide Sasquatch enthusiasts as to the best ways to find this elusive creature, we have listed, in no particular order, individual situations that are proven for different circumstances in our endeavors.

Sasquatch is the most sought-after creature on earth, and it has been forced to adapt to being constantly pursued by humans. It knows and uses every way humans can think of to find it, and dozens of ways we don't know!

FOOTPRINTS:

Although there are many known collections of plaster casts of obvious Sasquatch making, don't waste your time scanning the ground for them. Sasquatch has learned how excited man gets when coming onto a track, so now they have evolved; they only leave tracks when they want us to find them, and with only one purpose; to leave a false and misleading trail!

When Sasquatch travels, it seldom leaves any footprints, as it walks on trails where every footstep lands on grass or brush, thus leaving no evidence of its' passing.

Sasquatch habitat ranges across a huge territory in North America and Canada. Our many books contain encounters from all over the country, but our personal experiences occurred in the Pacific Northwest.

Thanks to contributors from across the continent, we have been able to discern from their personal experiences and our own, the habits and "tricks" that Sasquatch has been forced to develop in order to survive. This is not a means for the animal to merely avoid the nuisance of humans, but to survive the very many "Sasquatch hunters" who admit their desire to kill one! We won't go into the facts surrounding this very real threat, but the elaborate tricks that Sasquatch has developed to remain so elusive are for its very survival!

Sasquatch travels silently as our early Native Americans are reputed to have been so adept at doing. The creature steps first on the balls of its feet; unlike the white man who generally steps heel first; thus the "thump, thump" announces our presence. The Sasquatch walks like the human athletes and Native Americans do.

This fact was brought to our attention by a Native American friend and a contributor to our "Skinwalker" series; and in response to our surprise at the great silence with which Sasquatch walks and runs, he said, "That's why the white man is such a poor tracker; he looks, but he doesn't see!"

Once we accept the fact that when hiking in Sasquatch country, we can pretty much forget about carefully watching the ground before us and concentrate on the trail far ahead; that's where the best chance will be to see a Sasquatch.

Sasquatch has a habit of checking its "back trail," and does so on a regular basis. They do this more often when approaching the crest of a hill; the animal will step off the trail and preferably conceal itself behind a tree, and when in a thicker forest, they will often climb up a few feet. They will then carefully search their back trail for any sign of being followed.

If they should believe that there is a human behind them, they quickly run parallel to the hill's crest for far enough to the side where the grasses or trees are thick enough so that they can crawl over the top of the hill without being seen. Next, in most every case, the Sasquatch will watch for a while to try to grasp the intentions of its pursuer; and if the human continues to follow, the Sasquatch will disappear quickly.

When man is following this animal and crests the hill and finds it has left the trail, he immediately looks on both sides of the trail for signs the Sasquatch has made in the grasses. The Sasquatch being aware that it leaves a trail of crushed grasses will leave the trail in the following manner; first, it leaps to the side for several feet and when it lands, it turns back at an angle and travels twenty or so feet before it returns to its previously intended course and stays parallel to it for a ways.

Man is so attuned to his own travel habits that he continues on, looking for sign of a trail off to either right or left, and continuing at an angle in the direction he was heading. Sasquatch, in the meantime, is an eighth of a mile off to his left (or right) on a course parallel to him without his having a clue.

The Sasquatch also make it a point of being constantly aware of the location of the intruder; as periodically it will climb a tree in order to observe the current position of the human. Should man think, he should keep an eye out for any slight movement in the top of any large tree. Most hikers attribute any movement to a wind gust when in actuality it may be the Sasquatch!

An important point in this scenario brings out the habit of Sasquatch in keeping on its predetermined course. Always remember if you see a Sasquatch, mentally record its direction of travel, as it may take many turns and cutoffs, but it will almost every time, and no matter how long it takes, it will always get back on its predetermined route. This is a certainty!

This cutoff method for Sasquatch departing the established and "easy to walk on" trail, if often hard to spot; and it may take quite a bit of back and forth looking for it, but it will be of tremendous benefit to you, because you must know which side of the trail it exited on. If it cut off to your left for example, you now need to concentrate primarily on your left side for future observations, as it will be on a parallel course to yours almost every time.

Many hikers who see this "angled back" cutoff will get on the animals' trail as it takes this route of escape, however, it is not advisable, as the cunning animal will really make the going so rough, you'll soon give up further pursuit.

Climbing over a few dozen dead trees after this long-legged trickster will soon leave you far behind and exhausted. The main item of importance again, is to see on which side of you the animal left the trail.

Now, on rare occasions, the Sasquatch has been known to cross back over to the other side by gaining ground on its follower, but it is so unlikely, it's hardly worth consideration.

You may wish to increase your speed after once losing your quarry, because in many instances, and especially where the trail is not bare enough to leave many tracks, the Sasquatch will pick up speed to get far enough ahead of you in order that it may cut back onto the original trail and continue on its initial goal. You meanwhile, are getting a twitch in your neck by constantly looking to your left; when had you been aware, you might be traveling fast enough to catch it again. As previously stated, the Sasquatch will only rarely ever deviate from the direction in which it was originally headed.

As you may surmise, following a Sasquatch is pretty much a lost cause. You're trying to follow this long-legged beast in its own back yard; forgetaboudit! Now that we've covered that scenario, you have the picture. Finding Sasquatch is merely a matter of being in its known territory and being very lucky.

Getting back on trailing a Sasquatch; keep in mind that they have the habit of continually turning to observe their back trail.

At times, in areas where humans are more prevalent, Sasquatch will oftentimes make its way cautiously to the top of a hill, but before crossing over the crest, it will crawl to a tree, then sit behind the tree with its legs wrapped around the trunk and casually observe its back trail. Quite often when humans are about, the Sasquatch may stay on point for long periods of time in order to ascertain the person's intentions.

Almost unnoticeable, but you can occasionally spot the base on a particular tree where there is an unusual cluster of dark growth at its base; the Sasquatch sometimes allow themselves to get a bit over confident in their ability to fool us, and this larger than normal tree base may be looking right back at you!

SASQUATCH TEST:

Sasquatch has been known to spend a lot of time in observing humans. A lot like we would do if a Sasquatch suddenly appeared in a shopping mall, only the reaction would vary somewhat. When we are in the forests, quite often the Sasquatch will actually test our intentions. An animal that immediately garners man's full attention; seems to "test the water," as to whether it needs to run and hide, or just keep an eye on us. This test occurs generally by the sudden appearance of the Bigfoot, and it remains in sight only until it knows for certain that we have recognized it. After it has garnered our attention, it now steps behind cover and observes our reactions. If we should suddenly be heading in its direction with all sorts of scurrying, then it will shortly be gone. We therefore, need to harness our excitement.

If however, one simply pretends to not see the Sasquatch, the animal is likely to remain in the area, and if you then transition to an area out of the Sasquatch's sight, it will usually continue its previous activities; enabling us to stealthily sneak back into a position by which we may observe it.

Now, let's say that you are casually hiking on a seemingly normal trail and enjoying the wilderness experience; periodically step suddenly off the trail to observe your back trail. Do it quickly, and preferably in a spot where there is a growth of shorter pine trees, where when hidden behind them, no part of you is visible. Remain silent and keep any movement to an absolute minimum, and you may be amazed at what you see appear on the trail behind you!

Many varieties of animals seem to be curious about your intrusion into their homes. Every kind of creature has been seen following humans that use the basic precautions as they themselves do. From deer to porcupine, coyotes, even a pair of grey wolves; and the real prize is when you are rewarded by finding yourself eyeball to eyeball with a Sasquatch; do not move if at all possible! Any movement besides your eyeballs and the natural heaving of your chest as your excitement increases your heart's need for giant doses of oxygen will be a danger signal! Your careful observance of the Sasquatch will show that it reacts in much the same way as you are then doing.

Some Sasquatch will linger for many long seconds, allowing a long enough period for a quick study of each other. Sasquatch is as curious about us as we are of it! The natural similarity of bipedal animals is the "tie" that often will allow for much longer mutual observation. As long as no fear of harm is forewarned by sudden movement, or even the subtle stupidity of humans reaching for cameras, the friendly standoff can last several interesting minutes. Therefore, do not alter your original course until you have shown that you are not watching for anything in particular, and if the Sasquatch feels that you have not noticed it, you've bought some time.

Many people traveling through the wilder sections of the country spend an inordinate amount of time walking head down, looking for tracks and paying little attention to their surroundings. The fact that it is almost a foregone conclusion that you will not find the tracks of any Sasquatch; utilize your time searching the area with your eye out for anything out of the norm.

Pay closer attention to patches of evergreen trees, brush piles and heavy concentrations of berry bushes. Take a lesson from your Bigfoot brother and periodically step off the trail; preferably in an area of evergreens. Do so without first looking back over your shoulder as if you have an interest to pursue. Then do as the Sasquatch, and get behind and into the branches of that evergreen, and part them enough to enable yourself to watch your own back trail, and take time to see if something is following you. You may be amazed to see everything from deer and coyotes to Bigfoot itself!

Let's face it; our normal reaction is like the Halloween funhouse when confronted by the sudden assault by the angry witch; where we jerk, move quick out of shock and say stupid things like, "Hello!"

Prepare yourself in advance for a chance meeting with Sasquatch by believing in your ability to succeed in accomplishing this exact scenario, and you quite likely will be successful.

When it comes to Squatchin', there are no experts; only blind fool luck and carefully watching for anything out of the norm seem to be the keys!

SASQUATCH FACTS

Sasquatch is normally a rather docile animal. It is not considered to be dangerous when they are alone. Now, place that Sasquatch with a mate and/or offspring, and it's a whole new ballgame! The sound advice we offer in this latter situation is to immediately depart! Don't hesitate for a moment, not even if you have time for a photo, because your hesitation could very well cost you your life! This creature is not very aggressive unless it feels threatened; then, watch out!

All the female Sasquatch with its youngster needs to do is give one of her high-pitched shrieks and you will, within seconds, be facing the very definition of "terror" when the seven-foot tall daddy Sasquatch teaches you the true meaning of, "Run for your life!"

As one old timer friend of ours explains, "You cannot even imagine the horrible rage that can develop from a defensive Sasquatch buck!" Sasquatch has been known to loudly rage from such confrontations for long after the incident is over, and they have also been known to tear up trees, with root balls connected, and make horrible noises. Still, although making such ferocious displays, they rarely take out their anger toward humans, but instead; they leave an example of their displeasure in more dramatic, but less severe style!

Some sage advice for anyone coming "face to face" with a Sasquatch is to not look directly at it, but simply pass by, giving the animal the trail without any direct eye contact. Although this event is highly unlikely to occur, it has happened, and you must look straight ahead and pass each other in the same manner that the Sasquatch passes deer and elk. Eye contact in the animal world is always a sign of a challenge!

Most Sasquatch will avoid any possible contact with humans, however, in more remote areas not normally entered by man, it is possible that one may, on a rare occasion, be forced into a face to face meeting during storms or other events of nature; in such a case, pass quickly and quietly and try your best to "think like a deer!"

The basic etiquette of nature's creatures is that they most often pass peaceably if there is no necessity for confrontation, and the realization that there are "no enemies" among species in floods and forest fires.

Now should you find yourself in the very rare situation that has actually occurred in several remote areas, where you have met a Sasquatch on one of those trails where a meeting was inevitable, such as when rounding a cliff, where the trail was wide enough to pass, but barely; go quickly past without even a glance at the Bigfoot, and when past, go as fast as possible to put as much distance between you and it as you can. The reason being, that with the possibility of falling off a cliff is the uppermost concern at the time, because there is an unspoken rule that one deals with the most serious danger first and then goes to the next one. The key is to no longer be anywhere nearby when threat number one is past!

As has so often happened that we choose to mention it; keep going quickly and do not look back! There is a good chance that the animal's preoccupation with the danger of falling caused it to not even pay attention to notice what it was that it just passed, but now that it's gone by, perhaps the foreign smell of a human will suddenly and immediately cause the animal to turn and see what its subconscious mind had brought into focus. Now it turns to see if it has another challenge, as evidenced by you staring at it, things may get much more exciting!

The last thing you need to be doing at this point in time is staring at the animal, as from reports we have received from the field, the Sasquatch are perfectly willing to come charging back and attack!

One must remember that the Sasquatch is quite similar to us in the respect that it must deal with the severity of crises in order of the danger perceived. Therefore, in this scenario, the certainty of death by falling off the cliff is a given; whereas, under these circumstances, you have now become the only immediate threat!

There is only one thing for you to do now that this animal's adrenalin level is at its peak; don't look back, don't try for a quick photo, just get the hell away! We have been in situations where things suddenly turned ugly. The tide of passive tolerance turned to raging anger on the part of Sasquatch! Such actions are normally triggered by the human's propensity for talking "baby talk" to these giants. Obviously, they must have felt talked down to, because of the violent actions that followed; just like humans may do; ha!

This is another example that we strongly advise against. Keep in your mind the fact that confronting you is no big deal to Sasquatch. It has grown up seeing and learning to avoid humans. We are to them as rattlesnakes are to us; look and observe, but avoid! Now let's get back to being on a normal hike.

Let's say that you come upon a Sasquatch, and it cuts off the trail and runs cross country with you in hot pursuit when you lose it entirely. What now; tramp all over the area in hopes of picking up its trail again? No; simply retrace your own path by the flattened grass and get back on the main trail, because, unless the Sasquatch has been shot at or assaulted in some way; its rather simple mind will forget all about your insolent interruption of its day and return to its previous plan.

Get back on the trail where you left it and watch far ahead, and you very well may see the animal as it gets back on task. These animals are rather low-key and simple in their daily lives; they do not indicate any sign of advanced thought process, only a far superior development of survival skills. Sasquatch is obviously able to reason better than other animals, and thanks in part, to the growing human intrusion in its life, it has been forced to be even more inventive.

When following a Sasquatch, there is little need to be in too much of a hurry; in fact, it is often better to slow down somewhat. The Sasquatch will seldom ever get too far ahead of its pursuer. This will likely come as a revelation to many of you who have submitted your personal experiences to us in the past and expressed frustration with never being able to catch up to one. Fact being; if you follow the Sasquatch at a slower pace, it will stay the same distance in front of you, and it will continue to do so until you give up. When you consider this logic, it shows how intelligent an animal you're dealing with. It seems to have no desire or need to out distance a pursuer. The only exception is if you are in its home territory.

This discovery came out of a composite of so many sightings and pursuits, but when analyzed, it makes perfect sense; Sasquatch knows instinctively and through experiences learned from the adults as it grew up, that man will only chase it until he tires of the effort. Since man is out of his comfort zone in the forest; he always gives up if he cannot make visible progress.

Our analysis shows how very smart these beasts truly are, because they could easily outdistance their pursuer and continue about their business, however, then they wouldn't know for certain what their human adversary might be doing, or where they were. In that scenario, their advantage would be lost. Therefore, they will stay just so far ahead until man gives up further pursuit.

The proof of this theory was brought to light after we received several submissions from people who had, after long pursuits, climbed a tree to scout ahead for signs of their quarry, and there sat the Sasquatch on the trail ahead, calmly sitting, sometimes on a stump, and often in a tree watching them; as if it was all a game and waiting for them to catch up.

An important fact when tracking and following a Sasquatch is to know when you're being duped. The Sasquatch has learned through years of watching humans how wildly excited we become when on those extremely few times, we discover the "oh so rare" footprint! Humans tend to forget that, because our brains can multitask so efficiently, that our Sasquatch cousins are simplistic in nature; they eat, sleep, raise young and survive; period!

They have only the power of observation from which to ascertain our intentions and then to react to what instinct dictates. When they observe humans becoming so excited as they gather around the trail where the animal had just been, its fairly obvious that its tracks are the cause of all the flurry.

As previously discussed, the Sasquatch quickly learns that humans have a great interest in them, and as animals, they can only reason that our interest is to kill them and eat them, as any animal would!

No wild creature possesses the power to reason that perhaps another species would want to be their friends. Why would they? It's against nature!

So back to that Sasquatch footprint that generated all of that commotion; the Sasquatch is very aware that humans track it. For this reason, when you are traveling in Sasquatch areas and you suddenly find a perfect footprint that dwarfs your size twelve hiking shoe; be cautious! You have to slow down your heart rate and take the time to carefully scan the area around you. Could this footprint, the likes of which is almost imaginary in its perfection, have been purposely made?

Take the scenario where you have been following a trail for quite a while, and maybe you have become dangerously close to the hiding place of a mother Sasquatch with her newborn infant; perhaps her mate purposely left that all too obvious footprint to lure you away!

Now, no one with even half a brain would wish to knowingly discover the mother Sasquatch in this scenario, but it gives cause for thought; after literally hundreds of notations, letters, phone calls and face to face discussions with our Sasquatch story contributors, it is the unanimous consensus that if one finds such a perfect footprint so prominently displayed anywhere; it is a trick! The Sasquatch has purposely made such an easy to find print to lure you away from where you are not welcome.

The general rule of thumb, as taught us by a number of those contributors and friends, whom we consider to be personally familiar with the Sasquatch enough to be experts is; when you can plainly see the bare footprint and it is in your mind unmistakable; it is most likely there to divert your attention. They further advise one to begin a very deliberate search in a circle around that spot, keeping an eye out for a deeper print, even though blurred; which would be an indication that the Sasquatch leaped from making the obvious print off to the side. Once finding that deeper spot where it landed, which will usually be blurred out; a search from that landing area will usually turn up another trail, and that one will bear following. Sasquatch is a most proficient animal at leaving false trails!

To sum up the entire process and procedures regarding the possibility of tracking the Sasquatch; our suggestion is to instead; continually be scanning the areas ahead and to the sides, and you'll be far more likely to spot one of these beasts, as they oftentimes stand out dramatically against their surroundings. The odds of ever finding a footprint of Sasquatch are so remote that you'd be better served hanging cell phones from trees and hoping that a curious Sasquatch may accidentally take a "selfie."

You can hardly afford to divert your gaze from searching around you long enough to watch where you step; let alone looking for the Sasquatch print from the dumbest Bigfoot in the world! If the animal was so dumb as to leave any prints at all, its parents would have disposed of it long before, because any one of them so stupid would be a danger to them all!

So now, hopefully, you can forget about the forty pounds of plaster casting supplies you were hoping to use, and exponentially increase your odds of a sighting!

LET'S TALK "SCAT"

Perhaps a bit more time should be devoted to the droppings that normally help determine the identity of the animal. The Sasquatch however, is unlike other animals, as it has the ability to reason, and this trait seems to be inherent in every succeeding generation.

Unlike bear, coyote, wolves and others, who will normally just "stop and drop," or, as with the antlered species; they just "do number two on your shoe" if you're too close. Antlered game are a favorite, because they are so easy to track and they allow even a novice hunter to be successful.

Those in search of Sasquatch scat are up against a much superior intelligence, because, like humans, this animal seeks privacy. Whether it has any fear of embarrassment is doubtful, but it seldom ever does its duty in plain sight. It's almost as if it purposely hides it.

Normally, this animal lives in areas with an abundance of evergreen trees, and this is where the Sasquatch performs its act; it will seek out a short evergreen, back into its branches, parting them enough for it to squat down and leave its scat on the ground at the tree's base.

Since there are few credible Sasquatch experts out there that have spent any time in actual study, rather than in showy and erratic speculation, this subject has never seemed of any importance, but we feel it is important; "No scat!"

There are only a handful of the most serious professionals who are even aware of this trait; most likely due to the fact that very few people ever see a Sasquatch, and the effort of parting pine tree branches looking for poop is more exhausting than scanning the forests for a possible sighting of the beast itself.

We agree with this logic to a point; however, once a Sasquatch has been spotted or its existence in the area proven by a footprint, then it may be worth parting a few branches. This evidence of scat will only confirm that this Bigfoot may live nearby, however there is another factor of important consideration; and that is the fact that scat from Sasquatch is high in protein. This makes for an ideal food source for ants and other insects, and therefore the evidence has a limited time before the insects and the rains (which come more often in mountainous terrain) clean out the evidence.

The limited information we have on scat evidence from Sasquatch places it far down the list of clues, however with such an elusive creature, every bit helps!

THE EYES HAVE IT

There is a lot of speculation about the Sasquatch being primarily a nocturnal animal, but the main reason for this theory is that so few Sasquatch families are reported as being seen during full daylight hours.

Evidence has proven that the male Sasquatch is the primary provider/hunter for the family, and if there are young, then the male would be the one to bring food to the family while they will be sequestered in a protected and remote area.

This theory has also been fed by the fact that so many Sasquatch families are spotted after sunset and by travelers through our forests during darkness hours.

Many forestry employees and loggers report seeing families of Sasquatch in their headlights in both early mornings and evenings as they drive to and from work. It is reasonable to assume that these animals would be able to move freely after sunset without any intervention by humans, but easily spotted by their headlights; which is quite common, as these animals often use our roads for traveling at night, since there is no brush or obstacles to go around or over.

Multiple groups are occasionally come upon during the nighttime hours; presumably because even Sasquatch prefers the ease of our roads for its migration purposes, and it is a recorded fact that in the less remote areas, the Sasquatch normally relocate their entire villages about every six months. They are not known for these migrations except by a few dedicated researchers who have spent years studying them. They often relocate as far as ten or so miles. Therefore, our roads provide relatively safe passage.

We can easily understand the advantage of Sasquatch using our forest roads for nightly travel, due to the ease of walking long distances, and the fact that the first vehicle to come along the road will erase all evidence of their presence. Clever! No one knows how far these groups may travel, but some theorists have espoused that many of these moves can involve a great number of miles and many stopovers along the way. These relocations are a lot less common in the more remote areas where encroachment by humans is not an issue.

We have spoken to a number of ophthalmologists, who share their professional opinion that the Sasquatch most likely possesses superior night vision. Nighttime activity is certainly easy to accept. Not that this animal is more nocturnal, but suffice it to say, that even in the dark forest, it seems to travel at ease, avoiding the brush and easily stepping over downed trees that would waylay a human gives credence to the night vision theories.

To a person; experts agree that the Sasquatch has an uncanny ability to freely maneuver in the darkest hours. Perhaps nature intended this.

This could go far in explaining why these animals are so seldom ever seen during daylight. We strongly suspect that they are a semi-nocturnal species, although we defer to the experts who are yet to make any conclusion.

BIGFOOT TELEGRAPH

For those who have heard and otherwise experienced firsthand, the excitement generated by a sudden, loud "rap" echoing throughout the usual silence of the remote areas of our vast mountain and forest areas; it is both startling and exciting!

The first time we heard the "signal," it came as we were crossing a dry creek bed between two mountains in Southern Oregon. We knew instantly what it was, because we had been forewarned by area old timers. Still, the loud rap carried with it the realization that all of our studies prior to that moment were suddenly and dramatically proven; Sasquatch is real! (We had really wanted it to be.)

Our eyes met, and as if we had planned it in advance, we seemed to both share the same thought as we simultaneously sat down on large, smooth boulders that were alongside the now-docile stream that meandered through the darkening area where the mountains meet. As we glanced at one another, we shared that confident smile of confirmation of what so long had merely been a rumored and whispered about mystery, but now we knew!

Even though we had not seen the creature yet; the sound echoing from high above us was answered by a similar, only more muffled sound from a point further upstream from our location. We sat in silence, enjoying the back and forth communication between the two signaling parties, listening to the change of signals as one of them seemed to be continually changing tones, so we attributed this to the fact that it must have been going to meet the other one.

This being our first exposure to this Bigfoot telegraph, we then began our recording of information gathering; which years later, led to people sending us their stories of their personal Sasquatch encounters, which in turn led to our publishing a series of books including the collection of these encounters spread amongst them.

All along, we kept notes on the very few reports of what we began referring to as the "Bigfoot telegraph," and throughout our recording there seems to be an exceptionally varied and confusing group of signals used by these Bigfoot creatures according to the variance of terrain, and possibly a difference in signals was used by individual family units.

This accounts for a confusing number of variables; not only in signaling devices used, but also in deciphering a common meaning to the sounds. For this reason, we will discuss our consensus of opinions by those story contributors who have arrived at the conclusion that there is, "no actual standard." That is not what we had anticipated, but it's theirs, so we had to study a lot of varied raps and taps.

What we have is an amalgam of signals whose main intent is not to transmit any distinguishable message, but rather a sort of, "I am here, is anyone out there and would you like to meet?" What follows is the agreed upon and simplified "Bigfoot Telegraph Code."

First of all, the "signaler" most always prefers to send from a remote point where he (only the males do this) can observe the entire field before him. This spot is usually a ridge or hilltop of a higher point from where the sound will travel far among the surrounding mountains. These are not the monstrously high, snow-capped peaks that one might picture, but the massive numbers of smaller mountains as found in abundance in the "Coast Range" that runs the length of North America's Pacific Ocean coastline.

Sasquatch signals seem to be designed mainly to contact the local resident Sasquatch and are a means of obviously communicating among the various tribal groups that are known to exist. We have been able to discern that the altitude from which the signal is sent differs, as does the signal strength of the item struck, as to the intent of the sender.

For example; if a Sasquatch is simply checking to get a location of close companions, or to assemble a family group that are relatively nearby, the signal will not need to carry so far and thusly is most often made from a side hill or shorter hilltop.

These coastal mountain ranges are quite varied in the height of their mountains, and the individual family groups seem to usually settle in a place where there is a main or higher, dominant mountain, but their settlements will not normally surround this peak, but will instead, be in a semi-circle on one southern or south-western side of it.

This is obviously due to shelter from the extreme weather, and for the convenience of signaling; signals being always sent from a high point on the chosen mountain, but never from the top, so that only the individual tribes or groups under the chosen leader will hear the signal. This avoids the confusion of signals from other tribal units reaching those for whom it is unintended. The variety of signals sent are few, as they generally consist of a relatively simple testing to see how many are "out there" to begin with.

The preferred signaling device is a long-dead tree that has been topped by logging or lightning, where the center of the tree has rotted away. The center of the tree will decay first, and the outer shell will become even harder when assaulted by sun, rain and wind, until it eventually becomes the ideal "drum." A signal made by hitting the shell of this very tall drum can be heard for miles.

The signaler can determine how far and in what directions the sounds can be heard by the location of this dead tree. Downed logs that have often been further gutted by animals and wind can also make sounds that will carry for miles.

A consensus of opinions of experts have agreed that once the drum has been selected, the sender will normally strike this drum with a single rap. This rap will be repeated about every thirty to sixty seconds. This is obviously to give any responders adequate time to find a signaler of their own. Quite often, it is not all that easy to find a device near at hand, due to the extremely rugged terrain.

An example would be another Sasquatch further down the hill or mountain, in the midst of a healthy and sheltered growth of forest. A responder may need to resort to pounding a tree branch against a healthy tree or even a rock against another rock will suffice until the animal can find a better device for signaling, or if very close to the signaler, it merely heads in the direction of the sounds and sends a response at its earliest opportunity.

There is a need for a timely response, because the first sender may be traveling and stopping periodically to signal, therefore a rapid response is imperative so the first sender is still in range.

There seems to be no particular meaning to these signals except that the first one who initiates the signaling will have taken adequate time to select the best available drum and at a high enough altitude to be ideal for sending, so it will likely remain patient for quite some time awaiting a response.

The responder will return the same signal; that being a single tap. When the first signaler receives the single tap, it will answer the response with a single tap, and the respondent will once again signal one tap; one time!

From this point of acknowledgement by both parties, the usual next step will come again by the sender. The next signal will almost always be a set of two raps. This is a request for the responder to come to the sender.

If the responder is in agreement, it will return the two raps. From that moment on, the original sender will begin a series of single taps spaced quite far apart, that seem designed to be a directional guide to aid the responder in locating the sender. At this point, the meeting will eventually take place.

Now there is another response that has been documented. We have assumed that the first sender is looking for any Sasquatch in the area who happens to be within hearing; however, it perhaps is traveling with others of its family unit and this signal may just be a call to act as a locator to keep the group together, and we have not yet determined if different family groups may have their own personal signals among themselves. Some of our regular contributors have expressed this possibility, and are conducting ongoing studies of different family units, but this is likely to be a long study, as everything about these creatures seems to be.

We do have an example of two-way communication among them, as in the case where the first sender has, in response to the answering rap, sent back the two raps to get together, when instead of the similar two rap response from the responder, it sends back instead three raps. This signal has often been heard and it is believed to be a simple refusal for it to respond by climbing up to the sender. No determination has yet been agreed upon as to the reason, but the signal of three raps is usually followed within seconds by two more raps, again from the responding party.

This series in sequence seems to first be one rap, followed by a response of one rap, then the invitation from the sender of two raps, and then either an answering two raps from Sasquatch II which says, "I'm coming," or a three-rap refusal. Then the responder may itself, send a two-rap signal which means, "You come down to me."

There is an agreed upon consensus that if the original sender is in agreement to "come down," then the first sender sends out three raps and the situation is reversed in the fact that the responder then sends out a series of single raps that act as a directional signal to the upper Sasquatch to follow downward.

This at first was confusing, but when we consider that maybe the Sasquatch responder had made a kill and thus its refusal to go upward has turned into a "dinner invitation" to the first sender.

This situation is different where a family unit is hunting together, and the signal varies in the fact that the initial signal sent out is generated by the one making the kill; and then the signal is always three raps. These three raps are then acknowledged by single raps by all others in the party, and the one who made the kill begins sending out the directional single raps until all are gathered.

There have been a variety of other signals reported to us over the years, but those seem to be variations of sorts in different family units that have meaning to these individual groups that are common only to their particular clan or tribe.

The distance that the sounds of a hollow tree or log being struck can travel through the mountain is really surprising, and it takes one's breath away when you hear it and think of the monster that may be making it; especially so when you're miles from civilization and planning to spend the night in the dense forest!

ANOTHER SASQUATCH DECEPTION

This highly intelligent creature is fully aware of how excited humans become when they come upon sign of the Bigfoot; whether by sight or footprints. Since humans are aware that the Sasquatch is legitimate, it is natural to keep an eye out for the tracks and signs of the most fascinating animal of all time!

The Sasquatch has another newly discovered trick that has only recently come to light. The shrewd beast is always watching its back trail whenever it travels on trails and roads shared by humans, and it tries its best to not leave tracks.

Take for example, the reports we received from many reliable sources who are fortunate to have enough first-hand knowledge of Sasquatch!

Once Sasquatch is aware that humans have found its sign and are on its trail, they immediately react by hurrying further down the path to gain some time; then it looks for another animal trail cutting off from the one they are on; only one that is mostly in taller grass, such as a new deer trail. They will then pull the grasses from the place where this cutoff trail begins for about six feet or so, and then they will carefully step hard on the freshly made trail to leave their own footprints as clear and plainly visible as they can. Their next move is to walk a few feet on this deer trail, and then step off the trail, and taking huge leaps, they hop through the grasses and rejoin their original route once more while the humans wander aimlessly on the deer trails, where they assume Sasquatch is still ahead of them, as they are not aware that the Bigfoot leaped off into the grass.

This is so important, it bears repeating. Sasquatch will often leave clear footprints when they wish to "lose" their human trackers by leaving a plain footprint just before a grass covered, but obvious animal trail, as though they went that way. Then they jump off right away! If there is a nearby tree that you can climb, you will see the spot where the Sasquatch landed and then went back on its original course again.

These creatures are fully aware that humans consider them and their tracks as a matter of great curiosity, and many of our contributors have witnessed these clever deceptions. Many others who have long suspected these tricky maneuvers have verified similar cases of the Sasquatch suddenly disappearing. This is where the beasts quite often begin walking backwards and really confuse their pursuers!

As one who has watched many of these antics from his perch high in a pine tree put it, "Here they are; confused humans following deer trails leading every which-way across this entire grass covered mountain meadow, while the poor deer are dashing here and there trying to find a place to graze in peace. Meanwhile from my lofty observation post, I am watching a pair of Sasquatch casually cross over the hill and leisurely enter the valley on the opposite side of the ridge." All this, while the "Daniel Boone" wannabees are getting covered with brambles and stickers as they chase the confused deer. We suggest that our readers keep this trick of the Sasquatch in mind, as it is one they repeat over and over again!

These animals are very adept at traversing areas that will be a struggle to humans, but to their perspective, it is just a simple matter of seeing the trail better from their superior height.

They also know where to place their feet. For example; where a human will most always cross a hill to walk on the flat surface on top or along the bottom; the Sasquatch will most every time walk halfway up or halfway down every hill, and purposely walk sideways on the slope itself parallel to the ridge. The winds and gravity will soon obliterate the animal's passing, and humans rarely ever spot these trails.

Oftentimes when a Sasquatch is being pursued by humans, it will leave the trail it is on by taking the first deer trail that cuts off the main route; as deer so often do, as they prefer to travel through the grasses so they can graze as they travel. Sasquatch will stay on the deer trail until some point where it can conduct one of its famous "disappearing acts," which generally involves a sideways leap into a patch of thicker grass that often grows into clumps throughout the fields, and thus, they leave no sign visible to humans.

Then the cagey critter will travel a short way back in the direction it just came from to leave what appears as the tracks of an animal going in the opposite direction. At the first opportunity, when it can once again swing back around, it will do so. This maneuver will usually end up with the Sasquatch now walking parallel to the humans, but far enough away so as to not be seen by them.

When one considers the long legs of the Sasquatch, it is easy to see how effortlessly it can leap great distances into the grass where the humans can't possibly see its tracks even if only six or so feet away from them!

Man, on the other hand, has been concentrating on the harder to read footprints and may continue for quite some time until the trail once again gets on harder ground. The pursuer will usually be following the divots in the sand when suddenly, there before him the print is distinct once more, but it has changed into a deer! Meanwhile the Sasquatch is on the other side of the hill walking parallel to the human, and long gone!

You may be surprised at how many people really begin to have thoughts of werewolves and shapeshifters, and many make the assumption that they so closely tracked this Sasquatch from the very beginning, and the same set of tracks, that it had to have been magic!

Well, the deer continued straight and the Sasquatch has likely forgotten all about the human, as this has been a typical day with just another human trespasser out of their element.

This trick is quite common for Sasquatch, and since much of its habitat is capable of sustaining footprints, it often will make the additional effort when tracks can be seen, to slightly twist its feet when crossing more bare spots in order to blur its prints with little effort.

Since Sasquatch is a true "quadruped," with the aid of its extended reach with those long arms, it can also travel at rapid speed on all fours! This is what it will often do in areas of more open terrain where the wild grasses normally reach two or three feet high and cover the vast areas dotted with trees and shrubs. The Sasquatch can traverse such areas with incredible speed, and at the same time, leave tracks that are virtually impossible to identify, even as it crosses occasional bare spots.

The Bigfoot's similarity to humans goes deeper than merely a similar body shape; the animal seems to possess an almost human ability to comprehend, and most startlingly, to reason! It knows full well that humans are continually looking for its tracks, as is evidenced by its watching the excitement people show when studying the ground it just left.

It is suspicioned by some authorities that Sasquatch may have an extra joint in either their knees or ankles, as they can travel so fast for so far. Many native tribes, both in the continental United States and throughout British Columbia, often have spoken of the unique ability the Sasquatch possesses to be able to travel "between dimensions." They make reference to it as a "spirit being;" they say it possesses a "spirit aura." Experts interpret this as, "One damned smart animal!"

PHOTOGRAPHING SASQUATCH

The fact that there are so few photographs of Sasquatch intensifies the skepticism of its existence. This adds fuel to the non-believers, which is to Sasquatch's advantage.

When one considers the fact that the very rare encounters with Sasquatch normally occur when both humans and Sasquatch are totally engaged in some activity that has caused both parties to be immersed in their own thoughts, and voila; they meet!

The chances of coming face to face with a Bigfoot are so rare that no sane person is going to hike through our remote forests with camera in hand, just on the off-chance they may meet a Sasquatch. The areas in which these creatures live are not conducive to leisurely strolls where a person can walk in comfort as on a city park pathway. Instead, following animal trails in Sasquatch territory consists of placing every footstep cautiously to avoid rocks, roots, holes and slippery areas where one may easily trip and maybe break a foot, ankle or leg. In the remote areas, a misstep can cost a person their life!

Even with the case of traveling with a companion; and a person trips on a root or loose stone, the situation can, in seconds, turn disastrous. A sprained or broken ankle can be life-threatening, even when with someone else there. What can a companion do; carry you miles to where you entered the forest? Drag you? No; they are probably going to make you comfortable and go for help. So now what happens if you're in areas where wolves and cougars live? This is typical Sasquatch country.

Many people carry a handgun for protection, but if they are a "couple," it is highly unlikely they each carry one, so when they separate and one goes for help; who keeps the gun? Most people never give any forethought to these situations, but you'd better believe that when the night sky turns the forests totally dark on a cloud covered, cold night; that's when the fear sets in! A gun may not make you any warmer, but your shivering will at least not be from fear! It is amazing, the sounds the forest emits after dark; it gets downright eerie!

This type of scenario may be extremely rare, but having interviewed many people who have experienced these types of situations; most all of them admitted to feeling such intense fear that even thinking back on the event makes them shiver at the thought!

This is the longer version of our answer as to why the absence of Sasquatch photos. Anytime a person is out of their own environment, they must remain totally alert and watch their step!

A contributor recently told us that she had missed three opportunities to photograph a Sasquatch in the last two years, so she feels that it may work best to hang her camera on a tree with a note to Bigfoot requesting a "selfie!" Maybe it would work?

Another factor that adds to the difficulty is that the Sasquatch seldom gather in group habitat, they are constantly on the move, so the sophisticated photography equipment is a burden when a person is also on the move.

The point and shoot type of camera is a better option, but most will shut off after being turned on for an extended period, and when turned back on, the annoying buzzing or ringing will warn any animal in the vicinity that you are there!

We have on file, three separate reports from Bigfoot enthusiasts that tell of their sitting for most of an entire day at sheltered places near locations where Sasquatch footprints had previously been found with no success; yet when finally picking up to leave, two of them found fresh signs nearby of Sasquatch footprints, and one couple reported that one very large Bigfoot had suddenly bolted from a spot only yards away! All three couples stated that they believed the Sasquatch had settled in to see what the humans were up to; just how long they had been observed wasn't known.

According to another report from a lady hiking with her dog, said that a Sasquatch had followed them for miles. She had glanced back often at strategic spots along the trail where the animal was in view, but the dark forest in front of her prevented the Bigfoot from noticing that she was aware of its presence. The dog must have known of its presence, because she stated it kept glancing back with occasional low growls and whimpers.

Most people state that by fumbling with their camera, they lost that precise few seconds, and wished afterwards that they had simply concentrated on remembering every detail of the animal's presence, instead of scrambling for their cameras.

We have several reports on file where contributors tell of Sasquatch encounters where they fumbled for their cameras, and when they pulled them out, the eyes of the animal's widened, and where they had just been calmly observing each other seconds before; Sasquatch suddenly bolted in fear!

Kind of like the spaceman movies when all is well, until either the human or the alien suddenly produces an unknown object, and then it's like shouting "gun" when a police officer is nearby!

We humans should certainly be able to understand the effect that is mainly responsible for the almost total absence of Sasquatch photographs.

Put yourself in a public place; people shopping all around, when suddenly, you become aware of another person looking directly at you! How do you react? Well; men keep a wary eye on the other person while they try to recall if this could be an acquaintance. Women grip their purse tightly and instinctively move toward store security, or at least closer to male employees.

Now, put yourself in the forest and you suddenly make eye contact with a Sasquatch; what do you do? Let's say you're in a heavily treed forest and your attention is caught by a movement on your left, about a hundred yards ahead. You continue walking while warning your companion that you saw something "up ahead and on the left." What happens next? Nothing! Because the second your companion turned their attention toward the spot you directed them to, they sent a "confirmation signal." That's correct; when you first saw the Sasquatch, your body language gave ample evidence that you saw it, just by the subtle, but certainly noticeable eye contact and your long stare. Now you are visibly communicating with your companion, who immediately looks directly at the same spot. You just failed spy school! The chance is lost for a photo.

So, what should one do in this situation? First of all, the exhilaration and excitement of suddenly seeing a wild animal, such as a wolf or cougar, or most any of the "almost never" photographed creatures is enough to throw reason clear of the trail, but a Sasquatch? That's a whole new game! Very few things we can think of hold the excitement of coming face to face with the most elusive animal in North America.

Giving instructions on how to react in this situation is not even remotely possible, therefore we offer a consensus of opinions given by those contributors to our data base of knowledge; this is how.

Try to not maintain eye contact, and act as if you had not noticed the Sasquatch at all. Since it obviously has not been clever enough to conceal itself properly, you may just have found the lowest intellect one of its family. So, this could be your chance!

Keep walking without even a glance back at it, and try to keep your companion from noticing your excitement, but as you continue walking, slowly take out your camera and turn it on. If your companion has the camera, then you casually ask for it, but again, without a word about Sasquatch.

If you can still see the creature in your peripheral vision, pick your earliest moment possible, turn and begin clicking. Don't stop until it is totally out of sight, because the natural curiosity of the animal will oftentimes cause it to look back, and you may have another photo op just before it disappears from sight!

You may hear a, "Wish you'd have told me!" from your partner, but this way you may have a photo or two you can both see later.

We can all think of a time when we were being watched either by another person or by an animal, and the realization will most always cause a reaction from us; either as a change in our posture or a second look, but always a reaction.

This is the same, only more disconcerting to the Sasquatch, because when you compare it to how we react to a deer fawn, our reaction is magnified tenfold! There is no possible way to maintain your composure enough to tell your partner and relay this need to them without some perceivable reaction, so trust us, and when you get that prize-winning photo, please send us a copy!

Why not stationary cameras? That was our first question after being introduced to the mysterious beings that are the namesake of "Sasquatch Country." We both thought using stationary cameras would be a natural when our human mentors were tutoring us on the furtive creature that we had largely assumed was a localized "boogey man" to keep young children in line.

Since we had immediately began exploring our new home in the wild and beautiful mountains of Southern Oregon, we very soon had our first Sasquatch experience, and then the doors opened to us! It seemed that no one would ever speak to strangers about Sasquatch, and for the most part, they shunned any such publicity. The key to opening the doors to Bigfoot believers was obviously to have met one yourself before the locals would open up and accept you as one of their own.

After our first encounter we made a lot of new friends and we remember that one of the first questions we asked was, "Why aren't the forests loaded with those automatic game cameras on every tree?"

We soon were besieged with more answers than we expected, but it seems that the Sasquatch will immediately notice these cameras when they are attached to trees, fences or the like; and they either smash them to pieces with rocks or they must have a way of marking where they are placed to warn others, because there ends up being only a photo record of deer, humans, cows and birds, but no Sasquatch!

CAPTURING SASQUATCH

This is likely the most asked about subject when it comes to the elusive Sasquatch; so, let's explore the reasons as to why we don't have one somewhere in a zoo with so many other rare species.

When you consider the forces against such a venture, it helps us understand the mystery to a greater degree. First of all, let's analyze the enormity of such an undertaking. The costs would be horrendous; the organization would require the skills of a military operation, and to begin with, the entire project would not have a chance unless there was evidence of a Sasquatch presence within the perimeters of the research area.

This area would need to be cordoned off to prevent any possible escape by the Sasquatch. This factor alone would seem an impossibility due to the higher intelligence level of the animal, which would seem to be out of the question, as the nature of Sasquatch is that it doesn't make permanent settlements. Unlike other animals, it ranges wherever and whenever, and it maintains a constantly nomadic lifestyle.

Although the Sasquatch are known to gather in large numbers on rare occasions, they disperse after these short-term get-togethers and scatter in every direction. These rare get-togethers are largely assumed, by the experts, to be for the sole purpose of selecting mates, and there is no evidence that the animals maintain any sort of family relationships after these gatherings.

This lack of future attachment makes it more difficult for humans to understand, because of our tendency to maintain relationships among our extended families, and the Sasquatch seem to be devoid of such feelings, and any future family recognition or acknowledgement seems to not likely exist to any known degree.

As difficult as this may be for humans to accept may be explained because of the simple physical resemblance that we share. We never apply this idea of relationships to deer or other forest animals, so once we accept the fact that these are free-ranging animals with a higher intelligence level than the other creatures they live among; they are only highly intelligent animals.

Now it makes it easy to understand how difficult it would be to surround or capture these beings as it would be like "herding squirrels!"

When one considers the enormous costs and the amount of effort necessary to first ascertain the presence of Sasquatch in an area, and then immediately and totally seal off the entire area to prevent any chance of their escape, it would take more coordination and expense than one could imagine! Even the presence of parties planning the operation would cause the mass exodus of the entire animal population!

We have spoken to a great number of people who have seen and occasionally interacted with Sasquatch over many years, and the consensus of opinion is that these creatures seem perfectly content to live in areas they must necessarily share with humans, but they wish to maintain their fierce independence. They have no desire to make friends with humans whatsoever!

All of our many story submitters concur with the feeling that further attempts to capture or tame a Sasquatch could only hasten their demise!

HIBERNATION; TWO SCHOOLS OF THOUGHT

This question often comes up, and there are reports and theories that support both schools. It is theorized that some Sasquatch in colder climes may indeed hibernate; while those in more moderate climates may just need to increase their protein level by eating more meat.

This theory is exemplified by the black bear in southernly areas that do not hibernate, while their more northerly brothers do.

Some adhere to a sort of migration theory in those areas where the animals seem to possibly adjust their living area by an exodus southward during the coldest part of winter. This is the theory that many cryptozoologists have assigned to some Sasquatch.

Experts concur that less than 15 percent of a black bear's diet is made up of animal protein, while Bigfoot's diet is estimated to be around 40 to 50, or even 60 percent animal protein! This is thought to be due to their requirement to better nourish their highly functioning brains.

Sasquatch seem to acquire a larger stomach or gut area as weather gets colder, and this can be attributed to an enlarged digestive tract.

Not much is known about the Sasquatch's feeding habits in winter, due to the remoteness of their territories and the fact that they seem to become very nomadic, and often, whole villages of Sasquatch seem to virtually disappear!

Another factor that affects our wintertime reports is that neither humans nor Sasquatch seem to have much desire to tramp around and venture too far from their snug homes!

SASQUATCHS' HIDDEN HIGHWAYS

We finally answered a part of the mystery as to how such an enormous creature could live among our forests in relative anonymity. Our study of "tracking" in this book discloses the means that Sasquatch uses to confuse those who would attempt to follow its recently made trails and its clever deceptions.

Let's talk about the hidden pathways and trails that humans seldom, if ever, see; and if they do happen to find themselves walking on one, they almost never recognize the fact!

Since the Sasquatch has a higher intelligence level than any other wild animals known to exist, we cannot analyze its methods of travel in comparison to those other creatures. In order to properly investigate Sasquatch, we must accept the fact that it has an intellect much closer to our own, and we need to stop comparing it to these other species, and compare it instead to human thinking.

Sasquatch can't help the fact that it has an apparently superior ability trapped within the body of a common animal. Perhaps if this animal could speak our language it could be capable of learning to live among us as equals. Maybe it is a good thing that it cannot!

Let's look now at the basic element of tracking an animal that obviously knows we will do so if given the chance. We are continually scouring the ground for animal tracks as we hike. Hunters and casual hikers alike, are always on the lookout for signs of other animals if only for the excitement of knowing that "they're out there!" An astute observer of this trait, such as Sasquatch, knows exactly what we're doing!

The noticeable absence of obvious Sasquatch tracks are partially due to its awareness that the humans it observes are constantly walking head down, and it knows they're not looking for pretty rocks. Sasquatch therefore, doesn't leave any tracks!

Did you know that there are many separate "Sasquatch Highways" through our forests? Well, let's examine a few; first of all, the Sasquatch has adequate time in most of its habitats to prepare for the seasonal onslaught of humans. While we impatiently await the snow melt and the warming weather to once more allow us comfortable access to the forests and mountains, Sasquatch is already there; busy disguising its paths and highways.

We can all relate to changes in areas we love to travel throughout, where there have been landslides that obliterated the passes and trails that we have previously used. Many that we may have discovered late in the season and had made plans to continue our exploration at a future date when weather cut our further travel short. Now we are observing a whole new landscape, and all evidence of our exciting discovery has been erased!

Even though it is so obvious; The fact that humans do not often consider is the very real possibility that the Sasquatch may have purposely altered the landscape to discourage our further pursuit! Never forget that these animals live in this terrain their entire lives, and they have their favorite well-established routes through their homeland.

When one of their preferred routes of travel has been stumbled upon by a human, they do not totally abandon this trail if it is important to them; so they must, as the alternative, somehow prevent and discourage the humans from further access and deter their having any further interest in the entire area.

Merely placing rocks, logs or creating other roadblocks is not enough; they must destroy the route completely and create the image of the entire surrounding area as being impassable.

Fortunately, by spring, the drainage of snowmelt will allow more than adequate water to totally alter the landscape and erase all signs of anything that would attract further human interest in the area, and Sasquatch will channel that water to its advantage.

We have been amazed at the amount of effort these creatures will expend in altering the landscape! Enough so, that we have many times in our earlier explorations; even though having made copious notations of recognizable landmarks, have walked right past our intended goals into seemingly unfamiliar landscapes; totally oblivious and confused. How could it have so dramatically changed?

Often in Sasquatch country, there may be a wide variance of canyons leading off in many directions from a central juncture where they all come together. The simple altering of a few stream beds can, over a spring time, change things enough so as to totally confuse a returning explorer, even those who return with photos, maps and GPS coordinates to remind them of where they were planning to continue their travels.

A person may wonder at the tremendous amount of effort that the Sasquatch must have used to totally alter the landscape; and people often ask, "Why don't they just move?" The same thoughts might relate to the devastating forest fires that so often assault California, but as with the Sasquatch; they don't just leave, because it is their home!

Most of these changes that we have personally found upon returning to places of interest, and from the many reports received from our growing family of Sasquatch contributors, that once a person finds one of the Sasquatch Highways, is to practice being absolutely silent! Anything above a whisper may carry far enough to reach the ear of a Sasquatch; perhaps on post as a sentry, or perhaps the leader of a Sasquatch family headed directly toward you!

We have already discussed the various methods that the Sasquatch have for walking where they don't leave tracks, and in sandy country, their favorite pathways are along the bottoms of the vast number of sandy hills throughout these areas. They purposely wind around these hills, stepping on the very bottoms of the slopes, about eight inches from the bottom, so that with every step, the sands from above flow down and cover all evidence of their passing. This may at first seem like a much more time-consuming means of travel, but when you consider that this animal is seldom ever in a hurry, the additional ground it must cover serves two purposes; not only does it disguise all footprints, it also discourages all pursuit from humans. First of all, humans cannot understand why any animal would not travel directly from one point to another, so even if they should find a sign that resembles a footprint, they would dismiss it as coincidental, as common sense dictates it is unimportant.

The only animals ever in a big hurry when they travel are humans! After all, the animals are in their own element and they usually only travel to hunt or relocate, so they have plenty of time.

Humans however, are always on a time schedule, so any waste of this time to boringly follow tracks, limits their remaining time for the chance opportunity of stumbling over a hill and discovering a hidden Sasquatch village!

SASQUATCH HUNTERS

We have often voiced our opposition to those so called "Sasquatch Hunters." We will not publish any submissions where the story involves harm to these magnificent animals!

We do however, have several acquaintances with whom we occasionally correspond; one such hunter, although not having yet killed one, has only failed in bagging one because of financial constraints and the huge time costs involved.

This is a very expensive hobby when you devote so much time and assets in its pursuit. He does have a very interesting collection of plaster footprint casts and a couple of blurred, distant photos that are hard to not believe are the real thing!

Our hope is that if he eventually succeeds in finding one close up, that he shoots it only with his Leica!

SERIOUS SQUATCHIN'

When entering our forests for a trip of any sort on foot, there are basic cautions one must respect if your purpose it to observe wildlife, and a great deal more if the goal is to find Sasquatch!

Naturally, the degree to which one prepares is tantamount to the amount of success a person achieves; especially when going Squatchin'!

There are many levels of preparation, depending on how serious one is about actually succeeding in having a Sasquatch encounter. First, if this is a one-day adventure, you must realize that your chances of actually coming face to face with Bigfoot are highly unlikely, because of the time element alone.

Seldom do these creatures venture near enough to the closer proximities to humans in normal day-hiking areas, and then, only on the rarest occasions that it is not even worth speculating. Therefore, if one is to take full advantage of accomplishing any degree of success, a four-wheel drive vehicle is an absolute must. To even have a remote chance of ever seeing a Sasquatch from a distance, you first have to enter their "backyard!" To do so required being in this desired territory which is naturally farther from civilization. Not just in distance, but in difficulty. One of our own favorite areas was only eight miles up a mountain from a ranch where we began our treks.

To begin with, if you are planning to attempt success at finding Bigfoot, you must begin your trek early enough so that you are well within their mountainous terrain well before sunup. Don't worry so much about your engine noise, or headlights, or the dust cloud you're throwing into the air, but, do of course, slow down well before reaching your point of departure, so you don't have a trailing dust cloud that rises above you parking spot to send visual notification of your location for miles around!

A good rule of thumb to maximize your chances is to park when it's still dark. Sound carries far, but is misleading as to direction in the mountains, but dust is an instant locator which is a danger alert for all forest dwellers, but more so with Sasquatch.

We have had good success with our daytime hikes in Sasquatch territory by driving slowly in four-wheel drive mode on the smaller, single lane trails that permeate the Oregon, Washington and Northern California mining areas. These long abandoned, ancient gold mining roads are still intact due to the rocky content of the terrain, being such that the frequent rainstorms and springtime snowmelt does little more than deepen some ruts, but the four-wheel drive easily allows travel throughout these millions upon millions of acres in Sasquatch territory. We have also learned the same is true in any mountainous or heavily forested areas, such as in Colorado, Montana, Wyoming and Utah.

Take your time when nearing the place where you intend to park your vehicle, and at this point, be exceptionally careful to not gun your engine; and when parking, exercise extreme caution to not make undue noise when opening and closing your vehicle's doors; and keep your voices down! Even an accidental banging of a canteen against your vehicle's window can be like blowing your vehicle's horn.

You're wondering why; so, let's analyze the sudden change in caution. First of all, your engine noise has been heard by all of the creatures in the nearby forest the whole time you've been climbing the road to where you stopped. Why the caution now, is because up until this point, the noise of your vehicle has been intermingled with the sounds of the other vehicular traffic from the distant highways, which has all melded into a continual sound as far as the denizens of the forest were concerned. Now, your engine noise has only slightly diminished the composite noise of traffic; however, any foreign sound you make from now on will immediately alert every creature within earshot that "man is present!"

You see, the continual traffic noise is not a threat to these animals, because its always present and accepted. Any foreign sounds such as the slamming of a car door, sends a warning that will carry throughout the area. Even if other animals a quarter-mile away didn't hear it, they will be alerted to danger when the deer go loping by, and the birds come flying away from where you parked.

We make it a point to push our vehicle doors to a close and even lock them by hand in order to keep noise to a minimum. Remove your necessary items and keep any talking to a whisper. Maintain absolute stealth until you are well into the forest; and then, once you are past the place you parked and inside the trees, you may resume speaking above a whisper.

Once you are safely within the shelter of trees, even a mistake of making a human noise will be accepted by the creatures as okay. It is only your initial arrival that must be camouflaged, because all previous danger to these animals has come from that "parking area!"

If you are a cigarette smoker, no matter what, do not light one up! If you do, you may as well resume talking at normal levels and just have a nice hike, because you don't have to worry anymore about seeing the Sasquatch or any other animal for that matter, because you'll never see one!

Sasquatch will not even see you, nor will it be able to point you out to its offspring, because at the first whiff of your cigarette, your chances died! Before you ground out that butt (make sure of it), all forest dwellers were at least a mile away and moving farther away from you! Not only is fire the biggest danger sign to every creature in the forests, cigarettes themselves announce the presence of the second biggest danger! No, not lung cancer; man!

While on the subject, for those smokers (was one myself for many thousands of puffs); if you really want to increase your odds of seeing Sasquatch, shower heavily before leaving that morning and do not smoke anything after. Wear clean clothes (when I smoked, I'd leave a fresh change in the laundry room) and keep a supply of fresh air coming through your car so that smoke smell of your vehicle can't linger on your attire.

When you have parked and before venturing into the forest, make certain that any items like GPS trackers, cellphones, and wristwatch alerts are off. Keep voices low and watch your feet carefully, because a rock dislodged from the trail can send an alert for hundreds of feet. The residual effect can be felt by a deer that bolted at the sound of that rock and frightening a gray squirrel up a tree, which in turn, alerted the big Sasquatch that was just about to step onto the trail about a hundred feet directly in front of you! What a thrill that would have been if you had only worn those softer-soled hiking shoes that you left home in lieu of those expensive beauties on your feet now!

Not condemning quality gear, however, it seems that many outdoor clothing manufacturers are more into looks rather than functionality. Like those outdoor fashionable jackets with the bright colors that would be difficult to hide, even in the middle of a forest of oak and maple trees on a bright fall day.

Do not make the mistake of spending a lot of your time playing sleuth. You know the type; walking head down, hands clasped behind the back while meticulously studying the ground for fresh footprints of Sasquatch. These people that search so diligently must have read somewhere on how to distinguish different animal tracks, and they all too often become very excited and vocal as they call for their companions to join them in admiring and discussing their find.

Too bad they didn't glance up and over to their right, as they would have really been excited to see the look on the face of that curious Sasquatch mother leaning against the giant ponderosa pine tree with her hand over the mouth of her even more curious little boy Squatch who was watching big-eyed at the strange goings-on's by the humans!

After countless miles of hiking in a somewhat similar manner to this, we now largely ignore the trail we are on if it is in an area where humans frequent the trails. Being almost a foregone conclusion that the Sasquatch will almost, never-ever walk where it has any possibility of leaving a footprint, or even the remote chance of having a face-to-face encounter with humans! Sasquatch has quite effectively lessened the excitement humans have previously felt and openly expressed about its existence by becoming a lot more cautious in its travel when humans are about. Just as the hoofed and more docile four-legged prey, such as deer and elk move more cautiously when there are signs of cougar or the nightly calls of the mournful wolves that can change the entire complexion of the area involved, so have the Sasquatch done by being more careful in their choosing their favorite routes through the mountains they are known to frequent.

Unlike the past, where the frequent plaster casts of Sasquatch tracks would occasionally make the news; you don't hear about it anymore. Not too many people are willing to hike the mountains carrying fifty pounds of plaster "just in case," and since so many of those casts were admittedly fakes, it further discouraged these efforts as futile.

When one considers that the Sasquatch themselves have learned to be more careful in their travel, this has accounted for a major reduction in reported sightings, and this has all attributed to our conclusion that it is a waste of effort to scan the trails for footprints.

Our advice for your best chance of sighting Sasquatch is to keep camera at hand, walk as fast as you leisurely can without a chance of stumbling or tripping, and continually be watching for anything different on the trail ahead. Even an unusually dense patch of brush may indicate the presence of a Sasquatch hiding behind it and watching to see what made the sneezing sound it heard from you!

Keep a constant vigil for darker than usual patches higher up in pine trees, and continually be scanning the sides of the trail. Our reason for walking at a slightly faster pace than most hikers do, is because the denizens of these forests are used to hearing a human caused noise, and having a fair amount of time before the people come clomping through on the trail. Then, before they are completely hidden, here you come, unexpectedly fast and catch them off guard.

The old nonsense about going very slow and sneaking up on the unsuspecting Bigfoot is a total myth!

Humans can't sneak up on a snake, nor can we creep up on a crappie. Our only hope is to stumble onto a Sasquatch!

Aside from this advice, we suggest that you periodically step quickly off the trail at a place where you can remain well-hidden and just sit awhile. You may find on rare occasions that there are Sasquatch who are sometimes as curious as we are; keep your camera on and ready, as you may very rarely get a photo of the Sasquatch that is tracking you!

Good Squatchin'!

FIELD NOTES

ABOUT THE AUTHORS

Gary Swanson had spent 40 years in the Pacific Northwest before he and Wendy moved to Grants Pass, Oregon, where they enjoyed hiking throughout the spring, summer and fall months with their dogs. In addition to their love of hiking, they also enjoy history. Southern Oregon is full of history of gold mining, logging and fishing along the wild and scenic Rogue River; so for them, it had been a great place to research history, explore the countryside and hike all at the same time.

Although the Swansons are now hiking the deserts of Southern Utah; they are still publishing the true-life stories from their still growing family of contributors in Sasquatch Country.

They are currently receiving and publishing these Sasquatch encounters from people across the United States and British Columbia, and as far away at the now famous Oak Island, Nova Scotia.

Printed in Great Britain
by Amazon